T0195833

The Heavenly Blanket

Josephine Cioffi

Copyright © 2023 Josephine Cioffi.

All rights reserved. No part of this book may be used or reproduced by any means, graphic, electronic, or mechanical, including photocopying, recording, taping or by any information storage retrieval system without the written permission of the author except in the case of brief quotations embodied in critical articles and reviews.

WestBow Press books may be ordered through booksellers or by contacting:

WestBow Press
A Division of Thomas Nelson & Zondervan
1663 Liberty Drive
Bloomington, IN 47403
www.westbowpress.com
844-714-3454

Because of the dynamic nature of the Internet, any web addresses or links contained in this book may have changed since publication and may no longer be valid. The views expressed in this work are solely those of the author and do not necessarily reflect the views of the publisher, and the publisher hereby disclaims any responsibility for them.

Any people depicted in stock imagery provided by Getty Images are models, and such images are being used for illustrative purposes only.
Certain stock imagery © Getty Images.

ISBN: 978-1-6642-7238-5 (sc)
ISBN: 978-1-6642-7240-8 (hc)
ISBN: 978-1-6642-7239-2 (e)

Library of Congress Control Number: 2022912718

Print information available on the last page.

WestBow Press rev. date: 01/31/2023

This book is dedicated to my mother in heaven who inspired me to write this story. A special thanks to my supportive husband Jerry, my daughter Alessandra, my son Anthony and my father Giovanni. Most of all a special hug to my beautiful granddaughters Francesca and Liliana who have blessed me beyond measure. Grateful to Jesus for these precious gifts.

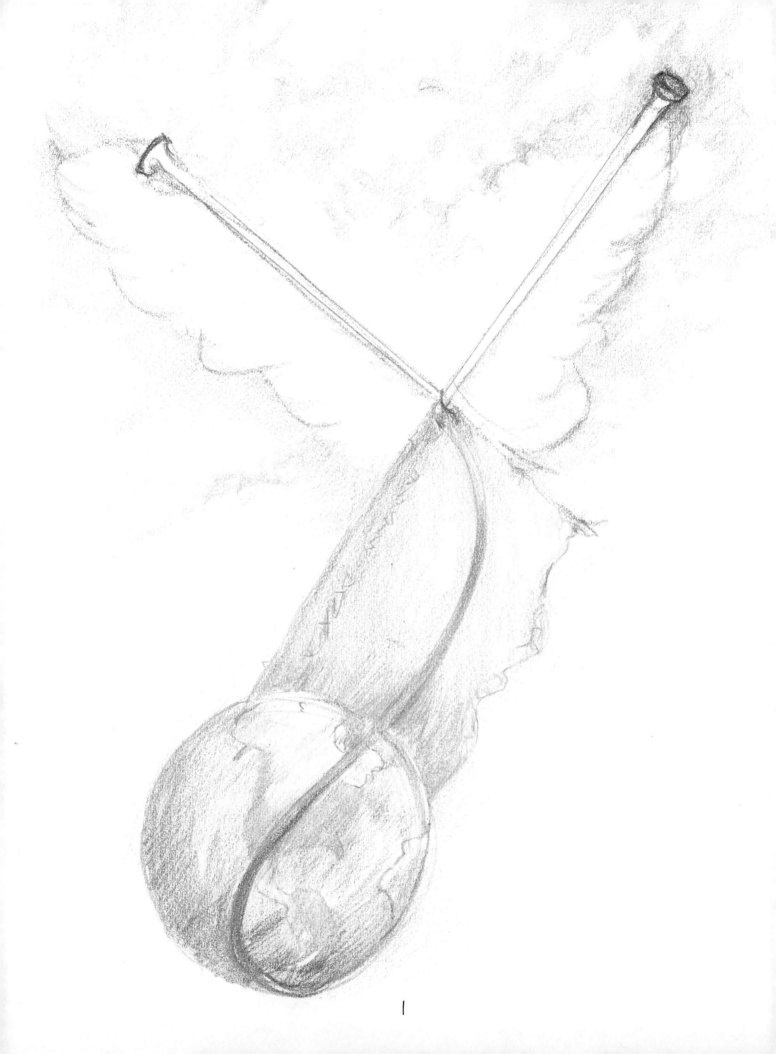

Dear Precious Child,

This is a story of a blanket sent from heaven above
from your bisnonna who was watching with love.

Although you didn't know her, she somehow knew you.
She wanted to meet you in person, but her time on earth flew.

You see, Bisnonna Teresa loved to knit and crochet So she made a blanket or two and tucked them away.

"Knit one, purl two," she used to say

As her needles began to click and sway.

A snuggly, cozy blanket was on its way

In hopes that it would make you warm someday.

"Another great grandchild is coming! Hooray, Hooray!"

Your mom remembered the love that Bisnonna put in her blankets. "Oh, how I wish I had one of those blankets for my sweet baby to love!" she said with a tear in her eye.

Your mom told Nonna Josephine who quickly said, "I will pray to Lord Jesus, maybe Bisnonna tucked one away."

One cold winter's morning Nonna Josephine went on a quest. She asked her father Giovanni, "Do you know if Mamma has any baby blankets that she may have left behind?"

"Look around," he said.

Nonna Josephine thought to herself, *It would be such a thrill to find one, if the Lord willed.* She looked in all the closets above and below. She emptied all the boxes and bins, but all she could find was a whole bunch of different things. *Except there were no blankets!* She looked in all the drawers, but one. Finally, she opened the last drawer. Much to her surprise, she found not one but two.

Bisnonna's beautiful handmade baby blankets were knitted with such love and care. "Thank you, Jesus," she exclaimed. "You have answered my prayers!"

You see, Lord Jesus hears us and loves us so much that when people we love are not here, he lets us know they are near and fills our hearts with love.

Much to Nonna's delight,
She found one pink and one yellow.
It was such a welcome sight.

WITH Tender Loving Care by Teresa Flecca

You hadn't arrived yet, so we didn't know if you would be a boy or a girl. How did she know to provide us with two? She wanted to make sure she could send you hugs and warmth, and a little heaven's touch. Each blanket had a special tag,

"Made with Tender Loving Care by Teresa Flecca," was her special sign.

She sent a warm snuggly blanket from above for you to call "mine."

As you snuggle in her blanket little baby, Know that
you will always be cuddled by her warm embrace.

With Love,
Nonna Josephine

About the Author

Josephine Cioffi is a Spanish and Italian teacher for the Springfield School District. She enjoys sharing the love of languages and culture with her students. She is born of immigrant parents both from the region of Calabria, Italy. She grew up with strong Italian traditions and values. Currently residing in New Jersey, she is a first-time children's book author and is looking forward to writing more children's books in the future. She is a wife, a mother of two amazing children and a grandmother to two beautiful granddaughters for whom this book is inspired.

Printed in the United States
by Baker & Taylor Publisher Services